The Student's Quick Punctuation Guide

A Simple Guide to Help Students Accurately Use Any Punctuation Mark

Tammy Black

GRAYSTONE PUBLICATIONS

Copyright © 2021 by Tammy Black

All rights reserved.

No part of this book may be reproduced, or stored in a retrieval system, or transmitted in any form or by any means, electronic, mechanical, photocopying, recording, or otherwise, without the express written permission of the publisher.

Published by Graystone Publications, LLC
Marietta, Georgia
www.graystonepublications.com

ISBN: 978-0-578-98034-8

DEDICATION

This book is dedicated to Grayson Black and students everywhere.

TABLE OF CONTENTS

A Note from the Author

1.	Apostrophes	1
2.	Brackets	5
3.	Colons	7
4.	Commas	9
5.	Ellipses	18
6.	Em Dashes	20
7.	Exclamation Points	22
8.	Hyphens	23
9.	Parentheses	27
10.	Periods	29
11.	Question Marks	31
12.	Quotation Marks	33
13.	Semicolons	37

About the Author 39

References 40

A NOTE FROM THE AUTHOR

I wrote this book for students to use as a quick reference guide on how to use punctuation in their academic writing. It follows the writing style suggestions from the Modern Language Association or MLA Style. If your instructor directed you to follow APA Style for your writing assignment, you should contact the American Psychological Association for guidance on APA Style punctuation.

,

1. APOSTROPHES

Apostrophes are used for the possessive case, for contractions and other omissions of words and letters, and for certain plural forms.

Using apostrophes for the possessive case of singular nouns and indefinite pronouns

The possessive case indicates ownership or possession of something by someone. Add an apostrophe and 's' to form the possessive of most singular nouns, including those that end in 's.'

Examples: My sister's grades have improved since she began studying with a tutor.

James's car was towed because he forgot to put money in the parking meter.

Use an apostrophe to form the possessive of indefinite pronouns.

Example: Anyone's dorm room key will also work for the laundry room.

Please note that you should not use an apostrophe with possessive forms of personal pronouns, i.e., yours, his, hers, its, ours, or theirs.

Using apostrophes for the possessive case of plural nouns

Add an apostrophe and 's' to plural nouns that don't end in 's.'

Example: The women's basketball team has a perfect record this season.

Only add an apostrophe to plural nouns ending in 's.'

Example: The seniors' portraits were hung in the lobby for the whole school to admire.

Using apostrophes for the possessive case of compound words

When using compound words, only make the last word in the group possessive.

Example: We watched the secretary of state's speech in my political science class.

Using apostrophes for the possessive case with two or more nouns

If you intend to indicate individual possession by two or more owners, make each noun possessive.

Example: There are vast differences between Jessica's and Mike's college entrance essays.

To indicate joint possession, make only the last noun possessive.

Example: Jenny and Christy's apartment is about three miles from their college campus.

Using apostrophes for contractions and other omissions

Contractions are combinations of words formed by eliminating certain letters, which is indicated by an apostrophe.

Examples:
- they are = they're
- do not = don't
- does not = doesn't
- was not = wasn't
- who is = who's
- you are = you're

Contractions are primarily used in conversation and informal writing. Most academic writing, however, discourages using contractions frequently.

Apostrophes also indicate omissions in some common phrases.

<u>Examples</u>:	ten of the clock = ten o'clock
rock and roll = rock 'n' roll
class of 2024 = class of '24

Using apostrophes to form plurals of numbers, letters, and symbols

Add an apostrophe and 's' to form the plural of numbers, letters, symbols, and words used as such.

<u>Examples</u>:	The gymnast needs scores of 8's and 9's to advance to the next round.

I must receive all a's this semester to graduate with honors.

It's important to read the fine print that is linked to *'s.

[ ]

2. BRACKETS

Brackets enclose explanatory words or comments that are inserted into a quotation. They also enclose additional information for material contained within parentheses.

Using brackets to enclose explanatory words in a quotation

Example: Jessica replied, "[Tiffany] didn't do well on [the test] because she failed to read all the assigned chapters."

The bracketed words replace the words 'she' and 'it' in the original quotation.

Using brackets to add to the information in parentheses

Example: Student-athletes must maintain a minimum grade point average (as determined by the National Collegiate Athletic Association [NCAA]) to continue playing their sport.

Brackets are used around the word 'sic' when the original writer misspells a word.

<u>Example</u>: In a letter to the editor of the school newspaper, one student wrote, "I disagree with the school's desision [sic] to cancel the concert because we worked hard to organize the event."

3. COLONS

Colons introduce lists or something that is an explanation or example of what precedes it. They also separate elements such as units of time or titles and subtitles. Only put one space after a colon.

Using a colon to introduce an explanation or example

Examples: Staying on top of your reading assignments is critical: if you wait until the last minute, you may not have time to finish them before the exam.

Each member of the sorority wore the same items of clothing to the pool party: a T-shirt, denim shorts, and flip-flops.

Using a colon to introduce a list

A colon can introduce a list of phrases, words, or clauses. A colon should only be used after an independent clause, meaning the clause can stand alone as a complete sentence. Also, it is unnecessary to use a colon after the word 'including' when it introduces a list.

THE STUDENT'S QUICK PUNCTUATION GUIDE

<u>Example</u>: My ice cream sundae came with three toppings: fudge sauce, whipped cream, and sprinkles.

<u>Incorrect</u>: The athletic department offers several sports for women, including: basketball, softball, and soccer.

<u>Correct</u>: The athletic department offers several sports for women, including basketball, softball, and soccer.

Using a colon to separate elements

Hours, minutes, and seconds:　　4:59 p.m.　　2:15:06

Titles and subtitles:　　American Literature:
　　　　　　　　　　　An Anthology of Classic Stories

Biblical chapters and verses:　　Deuteronomy 17:2

,

4. COMMAS

Commas separate parts of a sentence from one another and can indicate a pause in reading. Because commas often play different roles in a sentence, it's difficult to reduce their usage to hard and fast rules. The decision of whether to use a comma sometimes relates more to the purpose, rhythm, and style of a sentence than to a specific grammar rule. Students who want to master comma usage in their writing should not only learn these basic rules but also consider the stylistic decisions involving commas that you must sometimes make as a writer.

Using commas after introductory elements

A comma usually follows an introductory word, expression, or phrase.

Examples: Slowly, I made my way down the cafeteria food line, trying to decide if I should take a chance on the dinner selection or order a pizza.

In fact, only you can decide on the best career to pursue.

Sporting a bikini top and shorts, Stacey loaded her car with the beach essentials she would need for spring break.

Using a comma with a compound sentence

Use a comma before a coordinating conjunction (and, but, or, for, nor, so, yet) that joins two independent clauses.

Examples: I read three chapters from my biology textbook, and I completed the essay for my English class.

I planned to take classes this summer, but I decided to work at the bank instead.

If you use a comma between two independent clauses without including a coordinating conjunction, you'll create a comma splice, which is a grammatical error, so be sure to include the conjunction.

Incorrect: I'm terrified of speaking in public, I signed up for a speech class to help me conquer that fear.

Correct: I'm terrified of speaking in public, so I signed up for a speech class to help me conquer that fear.

Using commas to set off nonrestrictive clauses or words

Nonrestrictive clauses or words do not limit or restrict the meaning of the words they modify. They are set off from the rest of the sentence with commas. A nonrestrictive clause can be removed from a sentence and not change its main idea.

Examples: The students involved in the cheating scandal, who received perfect scores on their exams, will be expelled from school.

I forgot to return a book to the law school library, which cost me a $10.00 fine.

Restrictive clauses are not set off with commas because they cannot be removed from the sentence without affecting its meaning.

Examples: Students *who cheat on their exams* will be expelled from school.

The book *that I forgot to return to the law school library* cost me a $10.00 fine.

Using commas to separate items in a series

Commas are used between items in a series of three or more words, phrases, or clauses.

<u>Example</u>:   I carry a water bottle, snacks, and an umbrella in my backpack at all times.

Some writers choose to omit the comma after the next-to-last item in a series (often referred to as the 'serial' or 'Oxford' comma); however, students writing academic papers are encouraged to use it to avoid confusion. Notice how the meaning of the sentence below can change when the serial comma is omitted.

<u>With the serial comma</u>: I went to the party with my roommates, Mike, and John.

<u>Without the serial comma</u>:   I went to the party with my roommates, Mike and John.

In the sentence with the serial comma, it's clear that the writer went to the party with their roommates and also with a person named Mike and a person named John. In the sentence without the serial comma, it's unclear if they went to the party with their roommates and two other people or if they went with their roommates named Mike and John.

Using commas with appositives

Appositives rename a nearby noun or noun substitute. If an appositive only provides extra information and is not essential to identify what it renames, it should be set off with commas.

Example: Ms. Thomas, my high school art teacher, inspired my love of painting.

Using commas with parenthetical clauses

Because they often interrupt the flow of a sentence, parenthetical clauses that add information or comments are set off with commas.

Example: Rick's new car, it turns out, will have to be returned to the car dealership because it was recalled by the manufacturer.

Using commas with transitional words

Transitional words (i.e., 'however,' 'furthermore,' 'for example') connect parts of sentences and are usually set off with commas.

Example: Volunteering to serve as a resident advisor, for example, is a great way to get a discount on room and board.

Using commas with contrasting phrases

When a contrasting phrase is inserted into a sentence, it's offset by commas.

Example: It was the parents, not the graduating seniors, who were the most excited on graduation day.

Using commas with interjections

Interjections are words or phrases that express surprise or emotion, and they are set off by commas.

Example: My difficult algebra homework, alas, caused me to only get four hours of sleep last night.

Using commas with a direct address

Use commas to set off the name of a person or persons you are addressing directly.

Example: My friends, we must speak up if we want the administration to support us.

Using commas with tag questions

A tag question comes at the end of a sentence and is preceded by a comma.

Example: John didn't know today is your birthday, did he?

Commas with dates

Place a comma after the day of the week, the day of the month, and after the year.

Example: The Persian Gulf War began on Thursday, January 16, 1991, according to my history book.

Don't use a comma if the date is in inverted order or if you're only using the month and year.

Examples: 20 January 2021

My school was founded in November 1979.

Commas with addresses and places

Use a comma after the street name, city, and state for addresses that don't use a postal code. If a postal code appears after the state, do not use a comma before the postal code.

Examples: Portland, Oregon, is larger than Portland, Maine.

Please forward my mail to 1875 Pine Street, Arvada, Colorado 80004.

Commas with titles

Use a comma to set off a title such as Jr., or Ph.D., from the name preceding it and from the rest of the sentence.

Examples: My biochemistry professor, James Snowden, M.D., loves to tell us about his experience working in an emergency room.

Martin Luther King, Jr., was a great orator.

Using commas with quotations

Commas set off quotations from the words used to introduce or identify the source of the quotations and are always placed inside the closing quotation mark.

Example: "I want to go to law school," said Susan, "so, unfortunately, that means I have to take the LSAT."

Do not use a comma after a question mark or exclamation point in a quotation.

Example: "Do you want to go to the movies tonight?" asked Mark. "If not, we can stay in and order a pizza."

It's not necessary to use a comma when a quotation follows the word 'that' or when the rest of the sentence includes more than the words that introduce or identify the source of the quotation.

Examples: After scoring the game-winning shot, the basketball player humbly said that "it was a team effort."

People who say "Have a nice day" are being polite.

Don't use a comma before an indirect quotation because it's not the speaker's exact words.

Example: Jenny said that she doesn't want to attend graduate school after all.

. . .

5. ELLIPSES

Ellipses, or ellipsis points, indicate that something was omitted from a quotation, or they signal a pause or interruption. Ellipses are typed as three periods with spaces in between them.

Using an ellipsis to indicate an omission

Use an ellipsis to indicate that you left out part of a quotation.

Example: Original text: "The actors in the school play, which was a revival of *Grease*, did an exceptional job."

With an ellipsis: "The actors in the school play . . . did an exceptional job."

When using an ellipsis after a complete sentence, retain the closing punctuation mark.

Example: "I'm majoring in biochemistry. . . . Unfortunately, my university doesn't offer a pre-med major."

Using an ellipsis to indicate a pause or hesitation

<u>Example</u>: My chemistry professor's monotone voice is very . . . well, it puts me to sleep.

6. EM DASHES

Em dashes interrupt a sentence to insert comments or highlight particular content. Unlike parentheses, em dashes put more emphasis on the content they enclose. Please note that you should not put a space before or after an em dash.

Using an em dash to insert a comment

An em dash can be used to set off information that does not fit grammatically with the rest of a sentence.

Example: When you get accepted to my alma mater—I know you will—I'll take you to dinner to celebrate.

Using an em dash to emphasize explanatory content

Example: Jessica wants to major in one of the humanities—literature, philosophy, or history—so she will probably attend a liberal arts college.

Using an em dash to emphasize information at the end of a sentence

A single em dash at the end of a sentence is used for several reasons: to set off a comment, to explain or summarize what came before, or to indicate an interruption in speech.

Examples: I had always gotten good grades in math—until I took calculus.

    We only take two exams in our history class—one before fall break and another at the end of the semester.

    Are you ready to go to the—wait, is that the fire alarm?

!

7. EXCLAMATION POINTS

Exclamation points close sentences that show strong emotion or surprise.

Examples: I got a perfect score on my history exam!
            Watch out!

Do not use a period or comma after an exclamation point that ends a quotation.

Example: "If we win one more game, we'll play for the conference title!" shouted the football player.

Because they can distract readers, use exclamation points sparingly.

Also, the use of multiple exclamation points is not recommended in academic writing.

Inappropriate: We won the game!!!

Appropriate: We won the game!

8. HYPHENS

The basic function of a hyphen is to link words or parts of words. Using hyphens can be tricky because the rules don't always apply to every word. A dictionary may help you decide if you should hyphenate certain words, but sometimes you have to make that decision as the writer. Below are some basic rules for hyphen usage that will help you make that decision.

Hyphenating compound adjectives

The guiding principle for hyphenating adjectives made up of word combinations is to hyphenate most compound adjectives that precede a noun but not those that follow a noun.

Examples: In our shop class, we had to saw through a six-foot plank.

The plank we sawed through in our shop class was six feet long.

Don't hyphenate a combination of an adverb that ends in 'ly' and an adjective.

Example: After receiving a low grade on my first chemistry test, I decided to take a radically different approach when I studied for the next one.

Hyphenating coined compounds

Coined compounds are a group of words that would not normally be hyphenated but are linked together with hyphens because they're used in an unexpected way.

Example: When her little brother spilled grape juice on her favorite white sweater, Jean gave him a get-out-of-my-room-now look.

Hyphenating fractions and compound numbers

If you need to write out a fraction, use a hyphen to join the numerator and denominator.

Example: It's critical that I do well on this project because it's one-third of my grade in the class.

Use hyphens to spell out numbers from twenty-one to ninety-nine.

Using suspended hyphens

Compound words that share the same base word can be shortened with suspended hyphens.

Example: Each student should write an essay for him- or herself instead of hiring someone to write them.

Using hyphens with prefixes and suffixes

Although most words with prefixes or suffixes are written as one word, there are instances when you need a hyphen. When the base word is capitalized, use a hyphen after the prefix.

Example: Some people believe it's un-American to not celebrate Independence Day.

Use a hyphen after a prefix that comes before a numerical figure.

Example: Many advertisers believe that the under-25 age group is more influenced by technology than any other group.

The following prefixes and suffixes usually require a hyphen.

all-	all-state
ex- (former)	ex-husband
self-	self-possessed

quasi-	quasi-legislative
-elect	mayor-elect
-odd	fifty-odd
-some (approximately)	twenty-some

Use a hyphen with compound words.

Examples: pre-high school; pro-civil rights

A hyphen can be inserted into a word to change its meaning.

Examples: I'm not going to class today because I need to recover from the flu.

   I'm going to re-cover the cushions from my sofa because I can't afford to buy a new one.

Hyphens can also be inserted into words to separate confusing clusters of vowels and consonants.

Examples: anti-inflation; troll-like

( )

9. PARENTHESES

Parentheses are used to enclose minor or secondary information in a sentence. The information within the parentheses usually supplements, clarifies, or comments on the words that precede or follow it. Parentheses are also used with numbers and letters that introduce items in a list.

Using parentheses to insert minor information

Note that you may place a period either inside or outside a closing parenthesis, depending on whether the clause inside the parentheses is a complete sentence. Commas, however, are always placed outside a closing parenthesis.

Examples: The ice cream shop on campus has the best frozen yogurt in town (especially the chocolate flavor).

My English teacher also teaches dance classes at the local community college. (I discovered this when I took a salsa class there.)

> Most universities require students to maintain a minimum grade point average (usually 2.5), or they will be placed on academic probation.

If you use a question mark or exclamation point with the phase inside the parentheses, place it inside the closing parenthesis.

<u>Example</u>: I can't believe Melissa passed on a (free!) trip to Cancun.

Using parentheses for citations

Parentheses are used when citing reference information.

<u>Example</u>: The study participants showed no improvement in weight loss (Pritchard and Robinson, 2018).

Using parentheses to enclose numbers or letters in a list

If you use parentheses around numbers or letters placed before items in a list, don't forget to put a space after the closing parenthesis.

<u>Example</u>: Six states make up the New England region: (1) Maine, (2) Vermont, (3) New Hampshire, (4) Massachusetts, (5) Rhode Island, and (6) Connecticut.

10. PERIODS

Periods are used to end sentences and are included in certain abbreviations and initialisms.

Using a period to end a sentence

Periods close sentences that make statements and give mild commands.

Examples: My school's football team is ranked number one in our conference.
Never leave a space heater on when you are not in your dorm room.

Periods also close indirect questions.

Example: We all wonder who will win the election for class president.

Using periods in initials

Initials of a person's name are followed by a period and are separated by spaces.

Example: My English professor's name is T. F. Jones.

However, if initials are used to represent a person's full name, such as 'JFK' for 'John F. Kennedy,' no periods or spaces are necessary.

Using periods with abbreviations and acronyms

Many abbreviations use periods.

Examples:	Mr.	Jr.	Ph.D.
	Ms.	B.C.	M.D.
	Mrs.	etc.	Dr.
	A.M./a.m.	Fla.	R.N.

Note that some abbreviations don't require periods, for example, the two-letter postal abbreviations for state names, such as 'GA' (Georgia) and 'NC' (North Carolina).

Also, groups of initials that are pronounced separately and certain acronyms usually don't require periods after the letters, i.e., CIA, GE, AIDS, UNICEF.

If an abbreviation or initialism containing periods comes at the end of a sentence, it is unnecessary to add another period to end the sentence.

Example: We studied biology, physics, chemistry, etc.

11. QUESTION MARKS

Question marks close sentences that ask direct questions.

Example: Does the career center offer job placement assistance?

Indirect questions or requests, however, close with a period.

Examples: She asked me to walk with her to school tomorrow.

Would you please close the window.

If you use a question mark in a quotation, place the quotation mark after the question mark. A comma or period is not necessary after a question mark in a quotation.

Example: "What time does the cafeteria close on Sundays?" Jeff asked.

A question mark may be used in the middle of a sentence if a question is phrased before the sentence ends.

Example: Do I still have time to eat breakfast before class? she wondered after she woke up late.

" "

12. QUOTATION MARKS

Quotation marks tell readers that the words contained within them were spoken or written by someone other than the writer.

Using quotation marks to signal a direct quotation

Double quotation marks are used around a direct quotation.

Example: My roommate exclaimed, "Jeff finally asked me out on a date!"

Single quotation marks enclose a quotation within a quotation.

Example: "If you don't know the answer to a question," my professor wrote on my test, "do not write 'I don't know' on the line, just leave it blank."

Please note that you should not use quotation marks for indirect quotations because they are not someone's exact words.

Example: My father smiled and said that he would never forget his college days.

Using quotation marks for titles and definitions

Quotation marks enclose the titles of short poems, short stories, articles, essays, songs, chapters of books, website pages, unpublished lectures or speeches, and episodes of television, radio, and podcast shows.

Example: "How to Pick a College for Your Personality" was my favorite article from the magazine.

Definitions are sometimes set off with quotation marks.

Example: Translated literally from Latin, the term *et cetera* means "and the rest."

Using quotation marks to signal irony and invented words

Enclosing a word or phase in quotation marks can be a way of showing readers that you are using it ironically.

Example: The cafeteria's pre-Thanksgiving Day "feast" was dried-out turkey and canned vegetables.

Quotation marks can also be used to enclose words or phrases made up by the writer.

Example: My friend Jenny made up an exercise routine for our aerobics class that she calls "Jennycise."

Using quotation marks with other punctuation

Periods and commas go *before* closing quotation marks.

Example: "If you can find a way to turn your favorite hobby into a career," said my academic advisor, "your job won't feel like work."

Colons and semicolons go *after* closing quotation marks.

Examples: We were given a choice of paint for our dorm room in three different "colors": light beige, medium beige, or dark beige.

My favorite song as a kid was "Itsy Bitsy Spider"; I still smile whenever I hear it.

Question marks and exclamation points go *before* closing quotation marks if they are part of the quotation.

Examples: The football coach turned to the injured player and asked, "Are you sure you can make it through the game?"

"Yes!" Dena shouted when she received her acceptance letter.

If the question mark or exclamation point is not part of the quotation, place it *after* the closing quotation mark.

Examples: What is the theme of the essay "Technology's Effect on Academia"?

The funniest episode of that show is the one called "Craig Gets Arrested"!

;

13. SEMICOLONS

A semicolon links closely related independent clauses and separates items in a series.

Linking independent clauses with a semicolon

Independent clauses are those that can stand alone as complete sentences. A semicolon can be used instead of a period when the clauses are closely related and the writer wants to create a pause that's not quite as strong as a period.

Examples: I'm not looking forward to taking economics this semester; I heard the professor is really demanding.

Vote for Tim Hudson; he'll get the job done!

Separating items in a series with a semicolon

Commas usually separate items in a series, but when the items themselves contain punctuation, using a semicolon to separate them can make the sentence easier to read.

Example: Jason auditioned for the parts of Tim, a loner who keeps to himself; Rob, a basketball player; and Chris, the typical party animal.

Using semicolons with quotation marks

Semicolons should go outside closing quotation marks.

Examples: My mother's favorite phrase is "treat others like you'd want to be treated"; I find myself saying it too.

The nickname for that fraternity's house is "the sauna"; the name stuck after the air conditioner stopped working during a party.

ABOUT THE AUTHOR

Tammy Black is a professional proofreader and owner of Benchmark Proofreading. When she's not helping students, authors, and businesses perfect their writing, she enjoys baking and reading books on personal development. Tammy lives in Georgia with her husband and son. Please visit www.benchmarkproofreading.com for information about her proofreading services.

REFERENCES

The following books were used as references to compile some of the information contained in this guide.

Casagrande, June. *The Best Punctuation Book, Period*. Berkeley: Ten Speed Press, 2014.

Lunsford, Andrea A. *The St. Martin's Handbook: Eighth Edition*. Boston: Bedford/St. Martin's, 2017.

Made in the USA
Columbia, SC
11 March 2022